D1607086

Seasons ABC

Patricia Whitehouse

Heinemann Library

Chicago, Illinois

©2003 Reed Educational & Professional Publishing
Published by Heinemann Library,
an imprint of Reed Educational & Professional Publishing
Chicago, IL

Customer Service 888-454-2279
Visit our website at www.heinemannlibrary.com

Designed by Sue Emerson, Heinemann Library
Printed and bound in the U.S.A. by Lake Book

07 06 05 04 03
10 9 8 7 6 5 4 3 2 1

Library of Congress Cataloging-in-Publication Data
Whitehouse, Patricia, 1958–
    Seasons ABC / Patricia Whitehouse.
        p. cm. — (Seasons)
Includes index.
Summary: An alphabet book that features items associated with particular seasons, such as fall
when apples are picked and put into baskets or summer when it is hot and we eat ice cream.
    ISBN: 1-58810-895-3 (HC), 1-40340-539-5 (Pbk.)
    Seasons—Juvenile literature. 2. English language—Alphabet—Juvenile literature. [1. Seasons. 2. Alphabet.]
    I. Title. II. Seasons
    (Heinemann Library)
    QB637.4 .W48 2003
    428.1—dc21

                                2002001163

Acknowledgments
The author and publishers are grateful to the following for permission to reproduce copyright material:
p. 3 Mark E. Gibson/Corbis; p. 4 Robert A. Flischel/Mira.com; p. 5 Lori Adamski Peek/Stone/Getty Images; p. 6 John Gerlach/Visuals Unlimited; p. 7 Richard Pasley/Stock Boston; pp. 8, 15 Pictor International, Ltd./PictureQuest; p. 9 Comstock Images; p. 10 Susie Leavines/Mira.com; p. 11 Yellow Dog Productions/The Image Bank/Getty Images; p. 12 Doug Mazell/Index Stock Imagery, Inc.; p. 13 James Frank/Stock Connection/PictureQuest; p. 14 Jeff Greenberg/Photo Researchers, Inc.; p. 16 Ariel Skelley/Corbis Stock Market; p. 17 Peter Southwick/Stock Boston; p. 18 Brian Brake/Photo Researchers, Inc.; p. 19 Alan & Linda Detrick/Photo Researchers, Inc.; p. 20 Steve Callahan/Visuals Unlimited; p. 21 Keren Su/Stock Boston; p. 22 EyeWire Collection

Cover photographs (clockwise, from top left) by Richard Pasley/Stock Boston, Ed Gifford/Masterfile, Alan & Linda Detrick/Photo Researchers, Inc.
Photo research by Scott Braut

Every effort has been made to contact copyright holders of any material reproduced in this book. Any omissions will be rectified in subsequent printings if notice is given to the publisher.

Special thanks to our advisory panel for their help in the preparation of this book:

Eileen Day, Preschool Teacher
Chicago, IL

Ellen Dolmetsch, MLS
Wilmington, DE

Kathleen Gilbert,
Second Grade Teacher
Austin, TX

Sandra Gilbert,
Library Media Specialist
Houston, TX

Angela Leeper,
Educational Consultant
North Carolina Department
of Public Instruction
Raleigh, NC

Pam McDonald,
Reading Teacher
Winter Springs, FL

Melinda Murphy,
Library Media Specialist
Houston, TX

Some words are shown in bold, **like this.**
You can find them in the picture glossary on page 23.

A a   Apple
B b   Basket

People pick apples in the fall.

Sometimes they put them in
a basket.

C c Cold

Winter weather can be cold.

D d Dry
E e Ears

Boots will keep your feet dry.

A hat will keep your ears warm.

F f   Fall

In some places, leaves change color in the fall.

G g   Gold

Some fall leaves are gold.

Other fall leaves are red.

H h Hot

In most places, it is hot in the summer.

I i   Ice Cream

You can eat ice cream to cool off.

Jj July

The Fourth of July is a summer holiday.

There are **fireworks** on the Fourth of July.

Kk Kids
Ll Lake

In the summer, kids can swim in the lake.

Mm Mittens

Mittens will keep your hands warm in the winter.

N n Nose
O o Outside

Your nose might feel cold if you go outside in the winter!

P p   Pumpkins

You can pick pumpkins in the fall.

Q q Quietly
R r Rake

Leaves fall quietly to the ground.

Then, you can rake them up.

S s   Summer Sun

There are lots of plants in this summer garden.

Plants need sun to grow.

Tt Tomato

Tomatoes grow in summer.

When they turn red, they are ready to eat!

U u   Umbrella

It rains a lot in the spring.

People use umbrellas to stay dry.

V v   Violets

Violets are flowers that bloom in the spring.

W w Winter

In some places, it snows in the winter.

X x Extra Fur
Y y Yak

Some animals grow extra fur to keep warm in the winter.

Yaks are animals that grow extra fur.

Z z   Zephyr

A fresh summer breeze is called a zephyr.

Picture Glossary

fireworks
page 10

tomato
page 17

violets
page 19

yak
page 21

Note to Parents and Teachers

Using this book, children can practice alphabetic skills while learning interesting facts about the seasons. Together, read *Seasons ABC.* Say the names of the letters aloud, then say the target word, exaggerating the beginning of the word. For example, "/r/: Rrrr-ake." Can the child think of any other words that begin with the /r/ sound? (Although the letter x is not at the beginning of the word "extra," the /ks/ sound of the letter x is still prominent.) Try to sing the "ABC song," substituting the seasons alphabet words for the letters a, b, c, and so on.

Index